A GUIDE TO YOUR GOVERNMENT

Meet the PRESIDENT'S CABINET

By Michael Rajczak

Gareth Stevens
Publishing

Please visit our website, www.garethstevens.com. For a free color catalog of all our high-quality books, call toll free 1-800-542-2595 or fax 1-877-542-2596.

Library of Congress Cataloging-in-Publication Data

Rajczak, Michael.
 Meet the president's cabinet / Michael Rajczak.
    p. cm. — (A guide to your government)
 Includes index.
 ISBN 978-1-4339-7261-4 (pbk.)
 ISBN 978-1-4339-7262-1 (6-pack)
 ISBN 978-1-4339-7260-7 (library binding)
 1. Cabinet officers—United States—Juvenile literature. 2. Executive departments—United States—Juvenile literature. I. Title.
 JK611.R35 2012
 352.240973—dc23

                                2012006951

First Edition

Published in 2013 by
Gareth Stevens Publishing
111 East 14th Street, Suite 349
New York, NY 10003

Copyright © 2013 Gareth Stevens Publishing

Designer: Daniel Hosek
Editor: Kristen Rajczak

Photo credits: Cover, p. 1 Leslie E. Kossoff-Pool/Getty Images; p. 5 Saul Loeb/AFP/Getty Images; p. 7 FPG/Archive Photos/Getty Images; pp. 9 (main image), 27 (main image) Alex Wong/Getty Images; p. 9 (flag inset) MPI/Getty Images; p. 11 (main image) AFP/Getty Images; p. 11 (ship inset) Stocktrek/Getty Images; p. 13 David Paul Morris/Bloomberg/Getty Images; p. 15 (main image) Mark Wilson/Getty Images; p. 15 (Philadelphia Mint) Les Byerley/Shutterstock.com; p. 17 kavram/Shutterstock.com; p. 19 Kevork Djansezian/Getty Images; p. 20 courtesy choosemyplate.gov; p. 21 Onentaly/Shutterstock.com; p. 23 Eric Draper/Time & Life Pictures/Getty Images; p. 25 (main image) Tom Brakefield/Stockbyte/Getty Images; p. 25 (Veterans inset) Spencer Platt/Getty Images; p. 27 (inset) Chip Somodevilla/Getty Images; p. 29 Mario Tama/Getty Images.

Printed in the United States of America

CPSIA compliance information: Batch #CS12GS: For further information contact Gareth Stevens, New York, New York at 1-800-542-2595.

CONTENTS

What Is the Cabinet? 4

Washington's Cabinet 6

The Secretary of State 8

The Secretary of Defense 10

The Attorney General 12

The Secretary of the Treasury 14

The Secretary of the Interior 16

The Secretary of Homeland Security . . . 18

The Secretary of Agriculture 20

The Role of the Vice President 22

Other Cabinet Members 24

Cabinet-Level Officials 28

Glossary 30

For More Information 31

Index 32

Words in the glossary appear in **bold** type
the first time they are used in the text.

WHAT IS THE CABINET?

The executive branch of the federal government, which is headed by the president, includes the vice president and the president's cabinet. The cabinet is a group of people who advise the president. As of 2012, there are 15 cabinet members. Since running the country is a big job, each cabinet member heads a department within the executive branch. Each department has responsibilities, which include keeping the country safe, making sure there's safe food for citizens, and promoting good relationships with other countries.

The president appoints cabinet members he thinks will best lead these departments. However, the US Senate has to approve each. The Senate takes a careful look at each person. If senators think the person is qualified, they approve the president's choice. The Senate can also reject the appointment. The president then has to find a new candidate.

FEDERAL *Fact*

Except for the attorney general, the head of each executive department is referred to as "secretary." The attorney general is the main lawyer for the United States.

Many Advisors

The president has many other advisors outside the 15-member cabinet. He also has the vice president and seven other officials who are considered important. These people are referred to as cabinet-level officials, but they aren't actually part of the cabinet. High-ranking people in each cabinet department may also advise the president. President Andrew Jackson actually had two cabinets! One was the official cabinet, and the other was composed of friends and was called the "Kitchen Cabinet."

Anyone can be a cabinet member if he or she isn't serving in Congress or as another elected official at the same time. President Barack Obama's cabinet, pictured here, included both men and women, many of whom had held public office at one time.

WASHINGTON'S CABINET

The **Constitution** suggested the creation of a close group of presidential advisors who would be in charge of important parts of the executive branch. It was President George Washington who shaped how these advisors would be organized.

There were only four people in Washington's first cabinet. Thomas Jefferson agreed to be the secretary of state because he had great respect for Washington. Alexander Hamilton was named secretary of the treasury. His job was to create the Bank of the United States, establish an official currency, and make a plan to pay off debt. The secretary of war was Henry Knox, who fought alongside George Washington during the **American Revolution**. His job was to organize the army and navy. Edmund Randolph was the first United States attorney general.

FEDERAL *Fact*

George Washington held the first recorded cabinet meeting in 1791.

This picture shows the first cabinet meeting with George Washington. It shows Henry Knox, Thomas Jefferson, Edmund Randolph, Alexander Hamilton, and Washington.

The Changing Cabinet

In addition to the four original cabinet positions, the heads of 11 other executive departments are part of the cabinet today. These are the Departments of the Interior, Agriculture, Commerce, Labor, Health and Human Services, Housing and Urban Development, Transportation, Energy, Education, **Veterans** Affairs, and Homeland Security. In 1947, the Department of War became part of the Department of Defense. This change reflected the fact that the United States intended to be a peaceful nation that wouldn't always be at war.

THE SECRETARY OF STATE

The secretary of state is the president's advisor on foreign affairs. He or she has many duties. The secretary of state works out the details of treaties between the United States and other nations and advises the president about people who may make good ambassadors.

The secretary of state serves as the chief officer of the Department of State. This department issues **passports** to American citizens and checks the passports of people who want to enter our country. The secretary of state's job also includes making sure American citizens are safe in other countries. The Department of State keeps track of a variety of information concerning other nations. The secretary of state makes sure that the president has this up-to-the-minute information whenever he needs it.

FEDERAL *Fact*

Foreign affairs are matters involving the United States' relationships with other nations. This includes working together and sharing concerns.

World Traveler

The secretary of state is often the official representative of the United States. If the United States has a problem with another nation, often the president will send the secretary of state to meet with their leaders. Sometimes these meetings are at the **United Nations**, and sometimes they are on the other side of the world! The secretary of state may travel more miles each year than any other member of the United States government.

flag of the United Nations

The secretary of state often visits other nations to spread good will as well as to solve problems. Here, Secretary of State Hillary Clinton meets with Georgian president Mikheil Saakashvili in Washington, DC.

THE SECRETARY OF DEFENSE

The secretary of defense is the head of the Department of Defense. He or she advises the president about ways to keep the nation safe. To do this, the secretary and the Department of Defense are in charge of organizing the army, navy, air force, and marine corps. They manage more than 5,000 bases and offices. They oversee about 1.4 million active members of the nation's armed forces, as well as almost 750,000 nonmilitary workers, in every time zone and every climate around the world.

The president counts on the secretary of defense and the Department of Defense to be ready 24 hours a day to protect the United States. Part of this includes advising the president and Congress about the need for new equipment and resources at US bases around the world.

FEDERAL *Fact*

As commander in chief of the armed forces, the president makes the final decisions about sending American forces into action.

Safe and Up to Date

The secretary of defense and the Department of Defense are responsible for making sure that each member of the armed forces has what they need to do their job. As of September 2011, the navy had about 285 ships, including 61 destroyers and 53 submarines. The air force has about 5,600 aircraft.

Keeping these ships and aircraft up to date and safe, as well as providing weapons and protective gear to all soldiers, falls under the secretary of defense's job description.

The headquarters for the Department of Defense is a building with five sides called the Pentagon near Washington, DC.

THE ATTORNEY GENERAL

The attorney general is the head of the Department of Justice and the chief law enforcement officer of the federal government. He or she is the lawyer who represents the United States in all kinds of legal matters. In fact, the Justice Department is similar in some ways to a very large law office.

The Department of Justice has the power to bring criminal charges against individuals, companies, and even foreign countries. Sometimes, the attorney general argues cases in the **Supreme Court**. He or she also recommends people for Justice Department appointments, like US attorney positions.

The Federal Bureau of Investigation (FBI) is part of the Justice Department. This agency tracks down people who break the law. The attorney general may direct the FBI to find out information about criminal activity.

FEDERAL *Fact*

Because the job of attorney general had grown so big, Congress created the Department of Justice in 1870 to help carry out the duties of the attorney general.

FBI agents work with the Department of Justice to make sure companies and individuals are following US laws.

Justice for All

One of the Justice Department's duties is investigating crimes related to federal laws. One division is the Bureau of Alcohol, Tobacco, Firearms, and Explosives. This agency investigates criminal activity and monitors the firearms and explosives industry. The Civil Rights Division of the Department of Justice investigates cases that involve people who have had their rights as US citizens **violated**. The attorney general and the Justice Department oversee the nation's federal prisons as well.

13

THE SECRETARY OF THE TREASURY

The chief officer of the United States Department of the Treasury is the secretary of the treasury. The treasury handles the nation's money. The secretary of the treasury advises the president and Congress about what to do with money that comes into the treasury from taxes and fees. When the United States needs to borrow money, it's the Treasury Department that handles the arrangements.

The Department of the Treasury and the secretary of the treasury keep an eye on how money moves around the United States. The secretary monitors how banks are run and consumer safety, which means making sure people are buying and selling things in safe and legal ways. This department also works to prevent economic problems in the US and around the world.

FEDERAL Fact

The Internal Revenue Service, known as the IRS, is part of the Department of the Treasury. This agency is responsible for collecting taxes.

The Mints

Alexander Hamilton quickly established a national mint after becoming the first secretary of the treasury. Today, Denver, Colorado, and Philadelphia,

mint in Philadelphia

Pennsylvania, are home to two of the US Mints that make our coins. US Mints make about 4 to 10 billion coins every year. Two other mints make collectible coins. Much of the nation's gold reserves are kept at a closed facility at Fort Knox in Kentucky. There, the gold is made into bars.

The Treasury Department's Bureau of Engraving and Printing is responsible for making the nation's paper money. These bills are called Federal Reserve notes.

THE SECRETARY OF THE INTERIOR

The US Department of the Interior protects America's natural resources. The head of this department is the secretary of the interior. The secretary of the interior is concerned with everything from water conservation to how land is used. He or she uses this knowledge to advise the president and Congress about a wide variety of issues.

One of the jobs of the Department of the Interior is to take care of the nation's vast national parks system. The department also monitors fish and wildlife, and their **ecosystems**. If there are negative changes, it finds out why and tries to fix the problem. The US Geological Survey is part of the Interior Department, too. It uses the best science available to study our country's environments— from mountains and deserts to coasts and plains.

FEDERAL *Fact*

The Department of the Interior is responsible for the nation's relationship with Native American and Alaskan Native tribes. It provides aid to these nations and people in many ways, including investing millions of dollars into their schools.

The Department of the Interior protects the nation's natural resources, such as Yellowstone National Park, seen here.

Clean Water

You have the Department of the Interior to thank for your clean drinking water. The nation's water supply comes from lakes, rivers, and groundwater. Some activities of people, such as manufacturing, mining, and farming, can affect the quality of water. These activities also contribute to the overuse of our water. Many agencies within the Department of the Interior are working together to find ways to conserve water, both for citizens' use and for environmental reasons.

THE SECRETARY OF HOMELAND SECURITY

After the **terrorist** attacks on September 11, 2001, the government created the Department of Homeland Security, which is led by the secretary of homeland security. Its mission is to keep the nation safe by working to prevent terrorist attacks and strengthening any areas of the country or government that could be at risk for a terrorist attack.

The Department of Homeland Security advises the president and Congress on matters dealing with possible threats against the nation. It has put screening processes in place to make sure people coming into the nation don't want to cause harm. The Federal Emergency Management Agency (FEMA), US Coast Guard, and the **Secret Service** are part of the department, too. FEMA helps victims of natural disasters such as hurricanes, tornadoes, and earthquakes.

FEDERAL *Fact*

The Homeland Security Act of 2002 created the newest position in the president's cabinet: the secretary of homeland security.

TSA agents check travelers' belongings in airports to make sure no one brings anything dangerous on a plane.

Border Control

The Department of Homeland Security monitors the nation's borders. This includes the nation's borders with Canada and Mexico as well as people coming into the United States aboard airplanes and ships. Agencies within the department, such as the Transportation Security Administration (TSA), investigate every person who wants to come to the United States to work or live. Sometimes people come into the United States without permission and without being checked. These people are called illegal immigrants.

THE SECRETARY OF AGRICULTURE

The secretary of agriculture heads the United States Department of Agriculture (USDA). This department puts policies in place concerning farming, water, and food. It also collects information concerning the use of natural resources, such as the soil needed on farms.

You have safe food to eat because of the USDA. It also tests water quality in the wells, lakes, and rivers that supply the people who live in rural communities. The USDA is also responsible for addressing problems faced by farmers and others living outside of cities, including their finances. In addition, the secretary of agriculture, with the USDA, oversees the nation's school lunch program and advises the president and Congress about the nation's food supply and agriculture.

FEDERAL Fact

The USDA educates people about eating well. It was responsible for creating the MyPlate organizer, which illustrates how to eat a balanced diet.

The USDA helps farmers continue growing good, safe food.

Protecting the Trees

The United States Forest Service is an agency within the USDA. It manages the nation's 155 national forests and 20 national grasslands. One of the more popular policies of this agency is the Plant-A-Tree Program, started in 1983. Through this program, anyone can give money to have trees planted in a national forest. This practice helps preserve good soil and makes sure future generations have trees to enjoy and clean air to breathe.

THE ROLE OF THE VICE PRESIDENT

The Office of the Vice President is considered a cabinet-level position. Officially, the role of the vice president is to become president if the president dies, becomes too ill to continuing doing the job, resigns, or is removed from office. The vice president may be a close advisor of the president and often attends cabinet meetings. However, this wasn't always the case, because there are few specific duties given to the vice president in the Constitution.

Today, presidents rely on the special knowledge and talents of their vice presidents. The vice president often represents the president to foreign nations and gives speeches in support of government programs and policies. Recent vice presidents Al Gore, Dick Cheney, and Joe Biden have been considered foreign policy experts.

FEDERAL Fact

The Constitution states that the vice president serves as the President of the Senate. However, he can only cast a vote if there is a tie.

Vice President Dick Cheney, second from the left, often advised President George W. Bush, right, while in office.

Out of the Loop

The Office of the Vice President was once considered unimportant. The Constitution was unclear if the vice president was even part of the executive branch. Perhaps because of this, vice presidents weren't always kept informed. In fact, it wasn't until after President Franklin Roosevelt died that Vice President Harry Truman was told about the atomic bomb! President Jimmy Carter was the first president to give an office in the White House to his vice president, Walter Mondale, in 1977.

OTHER CABINET MEMBERS

The president relies on cabinet members for advice about improving Americans' lives. The secretary of education works with the Department of Education to improve student achievement, develop programs for financial aid, and make sure there's equal educational access for all.

The secretary of energy takes care of the nation's energy needs. Today, the Department of Energy is focused on developing renewable energy sources such as wind and solar power, as well as energy from oil, coal, natural gas, and nuclear sources.

The secretary of veterans affairs oversees the benefits, such as health care and education, given to the nation's veterans and their families. The Department of Veterans Affairs cares for members of the armed services who have been injured or disabled during their service to the nation.

FEDERAL *Fact*

The Department of Energy oversees the nation's 104 electricity-producing nuclear reactors.

Caring for Veterans

The practice of taking care of members of the armed forces who have been disabled while defending the nation goes back to before the American Revolution. The **Continental Congress** provided money to disabled soldiers. Many states began building medical facilities and veterans homes during the 1800s. Today, the Department of Veterans Affairs provides more than 1,000 veteran facilities—including hospitals, clinics, and nursing homes—for honored US veterans.

Department of
Veterans Affairs
Medical Center
New York, New York

The Sequoyah Nuclear Power Plant in Tennessee, pictured here, is under the direction of the Department of Energy.

While the health of Americans is the main concern of the secretary of health and human services, other cabinet members work to help and protect Americans, too. The secretary of transportation leads the Department of Transportation. Its mission is to keep travel safe on roads, in the air, and on the water.

The job of the secretary of commerce is to support job creation and economic growth. To do this, the Department of Commerce works with businesses, workers, and universities across the country. The secretary of labor, head of the Department of Labor, makes sure that workers and retired persons receive fair treatment.

The secretary of housing and urban development leads the Department of Housing and Urban Development in creating programs that give citizens safe and affordable housing.

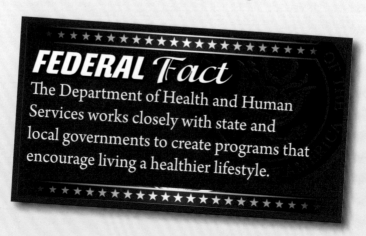

FEDERAL *Fact*
The Department of Health and Human Services works closely with state and local governments to create programs that encourage living a healthier lifestyle.

Cabinet members, such as Secretary of Labor Hilda Solis pictured here, often attend congressional committee meetings on topics related to their executive department.

The CDC

Have you ever had a flu shot? The **vaccine** used in this shot is developed each year by a key agency within the Department of Health and Human Services: the Centers for Disease Control and Prevention (CDC). The CDC conducts scientific research to find the best ways to treat illnesses. The CDC also works with the secretary of health and human services to make citizens aware of other health problems, such as heart disease.

CABINET-LEVEL OFFICIALS

A cabinet-level official is someone who doesn't head one of the 15 cabinet departments but has important responsibilities. These people are considered key advisors to the president and may attend cabinet meetings.

There are several cabinet-level positions. They include:

- White House chief of staff: manages the president's schedule while also serving as an advisor

- director of management and budget: assists the president in making the federal budget

- administrator of the Environmental Protection Agency: enforces the nation's clean air and water laws

- US ambassador to the United Nations: represents the United States at the United Nations

- US trade representative: advises the president on US trade agreements with other nations

- chairman of the Council of Economic Advisors: advises the president about the nation's economy

US ambassador to the UN Susan Rice speaks to member nations at the UN in 2010.

UNITED STATES

The US Ambassador to the UN

Each nation of the world has a representative at the United Nations. Its headquarters is in New York City. The US ambassador to the United Nations is the voice of the president to all these member nations. The ambassador relays the official position of the US government on a variety of important issues, such as global climate change, human rights, war, and poverty.

29

GLOSSARY

American Revolution: the war in which the colonies won their freedom from England (1775–1783)

Constitution: the piece of writing that states the laws of the United States

Continental Congress: the group of representatives that met during the American Revolution to help form the new nation

ecosystem: the living and nonliving things in an area that affect each other

passport: a government document that allows a citizen to leave their country and come back into it

Secret Service: the government agency that protects the president

Supreme Court: the highest court in the United States

terrorist: one who uses violence and fear to challenge an authority

United Nations: a group of nations that united after World War II to resolve conflicts between nations

vaccine: a shot that keeps a person from getting a disease

veteran: a person who was a member of the armed forces

violate: to do harm to

FOR MORE INFORMATION

Books

Landau, Elaine. *The President, Vice President, and Cabinet: A Look at the Executive Branch*. Minneapolis, MN: Lerner Publications, 2012.

Thorburn, Mark. *The President and the Executive Branch: How Our Nation Is Governed*. Berkeley Heights, NJ: Enslow Publishers, 2012.

Websites

The Cabinet
www.whitehouse.gov/administration/cabinet
Read more about the current cabinet and find links to each department's website.

The President's Cabinet
www.usconsulate.org.hk/pas/kids/cabinet.htm
Learn about the cabinet and other parts of the US government.

INDEX

ambassador to United Nations 28, 29

attorney general 4, 6, 12, 13

cabinet-level officials 5, 28, 29

Centers for Disease Control and Prevention (CDC) 27

Department of Commerce 7, 26

Department of Defense 7, 10, 11

Department of Education 7, 24

Department of Energy 7, 24, 25

Department of Health and Human Services 7, 26, 27

Department of Homeland Security 7, 18, 19

Department of Housing and Urban Development 7, 26

Department of Justice 12, 13

Department of Labor 7, 26

Department of State 8

Department of the Interior 7, 16, 17

Department of the Treasury 14, 15

Department of Transportation 7, 26

Department of Veterans Affairs 7, 24, 25

Department of War 7

Federal Bureau of Investigation (FBI) 12, 13

secretary of agriculture 20

secretary of commerce 26

secretary of defense 10, 11

secretary of education 24

secretary of energy 24

secretary of health and human services 26, 27

secretary of homeland security 18

secretary of housing and urban development 26

secretary of labor 26, 27

secretary of state 6, 8, 9

secretary of the interior 16

secretary of the treasury 6, 14, 15

secretary of transportation 26

secretary of veterans affairs 24

secretary of war 6

Transportation Security Administration (TSA) 19

United States Department of Agriculture (USDA) 7, 20, 21

vice president 4, 5, 22, 23